The Journal of William Dowsing of Stratford, Parliamentary Visitor

It has been thought that the following curious composition would form a suitable appendix to Dr. Wells's work on decorating churches. Not the least interesting remark which it suggests is, that the mutilations, to which our churches have visibly been subjected, were not the work of the Reformation, which would give them a certain authority in the eyes of Protestants, but are to be referred to the Rebellion in the next century, a political and ecclesiastical catastrophe which went far indeed beyond the wishes and intentions of the Reformers.

PREFACE.

THE original MS. of the following Journal was sold, together with the Library of Samuel Dowsing, son of the Visitor, to Mr. Huse, Bookseller, at Exeter 'Change, in the Strand, London, in 1704. At that time the copy was transcribed, with the consent of Mr. Huse, from which the present publication was drawn. The Editors of the Suffolk Traveller, second edition, p. 39, mention, that " part of William Dowsing's Journal accidentally came into their hands," which was dated 1648. A small error in their chronology I beg leave to rectify. The Earl of Manchester (under whose warrant the Visitors acted) received his Commission as General of the associated Eastern counties, so early as 1642, and resigned it in 1645, according to Clarendon, Rapin, &c. Further, to confirm this assertion, " In August, 1641, there was an order published by the House of Commons for the taking away all scandalous pictures out of Churches, in which there was more intended by the Authors than at first their instruments understood, until instructed by private information how far the people were to enlarge the meaning."—Mercurius Rusticus, page 22.

In this age of inquiry, any attempt towards illustrating authentic history is favourably received. Should this trifle meet with public approbation, the Editor's wish will be amply gratified in having rescued it from oblivion.

Woodbridge, May 15, 1786.

INTRODUCTION.

"TOWARD the latter end of the reign of Henry VIII. and throughout the whole reign of Edward VI. and in the beginning of Queen Elizabeth, certain persons, of every county, were put in authority to pull down, and cast out of all churches, roods, graven images, shrines with their relics, to which the ignorant people came flocking in adoration. Or any thing else which (punctually) tended to idolatry and superstition. Under colour of this their commission and in their too forward zeal, they rooted up and battered down crosses in churches and churchyards, as also in other public places; they defaced and brake down the images of kings, princes, and noble estates, erected, set up, or pourtrayed, for the only memory of them to posterity, and not for any religious honour; they cracked a-pieces the glass windows wherein the effigies of our blessed Saviour hanging on the cross, or any one of His saints, was depictured; or otherwise turned up their heels into the place where their heads used to be fixed, as I have seen in the windows of some of our country churches. They despoiled churches of their copes, vestments, amices, rich hangings, and all other ornaments whereupon the story or the portrature of Christ himself, or of any saint or martyr, was delineated, wrought, or embroidered; leaving religion naked, bare, and unclad."———

"But the foulest and most inhuman action of those times, was the violation of funeral monuments. Marbles which covered the dead were digged up and put to other uses, tombs hacked and hewn a-pieces; images, or representations of the defunct, broken, erased, cut, or dismembered; inscriptions or epitaphs, especially if they began with an *orate pro anima*, or concluded with *cujus animæ propitietur Deus*. For greediness of the brass, or for that they were thought to be antichristian, pulled out from the sepulchres, and purloined; dead carcasses, for gain of their stone or leaden coffins, cast out of their graves, notwithstanding this request, cut or engraven upon them, *propter miserecordiam Jesu requiescant in pace.*"—Weever's Discourse on Funeral Monuments, p. 50, 51.

What was thought to be left unfinished by

those persons then in power, the fanatical zeal of the succeeding century pretty fully accomplished; a reference to this Journal alone is sufficient to shew how far the ignorance and obstinacy of selfish men may be persisted in, and carried on, against the remonstrances of sober and moderate reason.

A TRUE COPY OF A MANUSCRIPT

Found in the Library of Mr. Samuel Dowsing of Stratford, being written by his Father, William Dowsing's own hand, carefully and almost literally transcribed, Sept. 5th, 1704.

WILLIAM DOWSING SUBSTITUTES

Edmund Blomfield of Aspell-Stoneham,

Edmund Mayhew of Gosbeck,

Thomas Denning,

Mr. Thomas Westhorp of Hunden (a godly man,)

Mr. Thomas Glanfield of Gosbrock,

Frances Verden for Wangford, Suthelham, Blything, Bosmere, Sudbury, Clare, Fordham, Blacksmere, and would have had Hartsmere.

Francis Jessup of Beccles for Lethergland and Shutford Hundred, Bungay, Blithborough, Yoxford and Ringshall.

THE
JOURNAL, &c.

SUDBURY, Suffolk. Peter's Parish. Jan. the 9th, 1643. We brake down a picture of God the Father, two crucifix's and pictures of Christ, about an hundred in all; and gave order to take down a cross off the steeple, and diverse angels, twenty at least, on the roof of the church.

SUDBURY, Gregory Parish. Jan. the 9th. We brake down ten mighty great angels in glass, in all eighty.

ALHALLOWS, Jan. the 9th. We brake about twenty superstitious pictures, and took up thirty brazen superstitious inscriptions, *ora pro nobis*, and "Pray for the soul," &c.

1. SUFFOLK. At HAVER^L Jan. the 6th. 1643. We brake down about an hundred superstitious pictures, and seven fryars hugging a nun, and the picture of God and Christ, and diverse others very superstitious; and two hundred had been broke down before I came. We-took away two

popish inscriptions with *ora pro nobis;* and we beat down a great stoneing cross on the top of the church.

2. At CLARE, Jan. the 6th. We brake down one thousand pictures superstitious; I brake down two hundred; three of God the Father and three of Christ, and the Holy Lamb, and three of the Holy Ghost like a dove with wings; and the twelve Apostles were carved in wood on the top of the roof, which we gave order to take down; and twenty cherubims to be taken down; and the sun and moon in the east window, by the king's arms, to be taken down.

3. HUNDEN, Jan. the 6th. We brake down thirty superstitious pictures; and we took up three popish inscriptions in brass, *ora pro nobis* on them; and we gave order for the levelling the steps.

4. WIXO, Jan. the 6th. We brake a picture, and gave order for levelling the steps.

5. WITHERSFIELD, Jan. the 6th. We brake down a crucifix, and sixty superstitious pictures; and gave order for the levelling the steps in the chancel.

6. STOKE-NAYLAND, Jan. the 19th. We brake down an hundred superstitious pictures; and took up seven superstitious inscriptions on the gravestones, *ora pro nobis*, &c.

7. NAYLAND, SUFF. Jan. the 19th, 1643. We brake down thirty superstitious pictures, and gave

order for the taking down a cross on the steeple: we took up two popish inscriptions, *ora pro nobis*, &c.

8. RAYDEN, Jan. the 20th. We brake down a crucifix, and twelve superstitious pictures, and a popish inscription, *ora pro nobis*, &c.

9. HOUGHTON, Jan. the 20th. We brake six superstitious pictures.

10. BARHAM, Jan. the 22nd. We brake down the twelve Apostles in the chancel, and six superstitious more there; and eight in the church, one a lamb with a cross X on the back; and digged down the steps; and took up four superstitious inscriptions of brass, one of them *Jesu, Fili Dei, miserere mei*, and *O mater Dei, memento mei*, "O mother of God, have mercy on me!"

11. CLAYDEN, Jan. the 22nd. We brake down three superstitious pictures, and gave order to take down three crosses of the steeple and one of the chancel.

12. CODDENHAM, Jan. the 22nd. We gave order for taking down three crosses of the steeple and one of the chancel.

13. YKE, Jan. 23rd. We brake down twenty-five superstitious pictures, and took up a superstitious inscription.

14. DUNSTALL, Jan. the 23rd. We brake down sixty superstitious pictures, and broke in pieces the rails, and gave order to pull down the steps.

15. ALDBOROUGH, Jan. the 24th. We gave order for taking down twenty cherubims and thirty-eight pictures; which their lecturer, Mr. Swayn, (a godly man,) undertook, and their captain, Mr. Johnson.

16. ORFORD, Jan. the 25th. We brake down twenty-eight superstitious pictures, and took up eleven popish inscriptions in brass; and gave order for digging up the steps, and taking of two crosses off the steeple of the church, and one of the chancel, in all four.

17. SNAPE, Jan. the 25th. We brake down four popish pictures, and took up four inscriptions of brass, of *ora pro nobis*, &c.

18. STANSTED, Jan. the 25th. We brake down six superstitious pictures, and took up a popish inscription in brass.

19. SAXMUNDHAM, Jan. the 26th. We took up two superstitious inscriptions in brass.

20. KELSHALL, Jan. the 26th. We brake down six superstitious pictures, and took up twelve popish inscriptions in brass, and gave order to level the chancel and taking down a cross.

21. CARLETON, Jan. the 26th. We brake down ten superstitious pictures, and took up six popish inscriptions in brass, and gave order to level the chancel.

22. FARNHAM, Jan. the 26th. We took up a popish inscription in brass.

23. STRATFORD. We brake down six superstitious pictures.

24. WICKHAM, Jan. the 26th. We brake down fifteen popish pictures of Angels and S^{ts}, and gave order for taking two crosses; one on the steeple, and the second on the church.

25. SUDBURNE, Jan. the 26th. We brake down six pictures, and gave order for the taking down of a cross on the steeple, and the steps to be levelled.

26. [a] UFFORD, Jan. the 27th. We brake down thirty superstitious pictures, and gave direction to take down thirty-seven more; and forty cherubims to be taken down of wood, and the chancel levelled. There was a picture of Christ on the cross, and God the Father above it; and left thirty-seven superstitious pictures to be taken down; and took up six superstitious inscriptions in brass.

27. WOODBRIDGE, Jan. the 27th. We took down two superstitious inscriptions in brass, and gave order to take down thirty superstitious pictures.

28. KESGRAVE, Jan. the 27th. We took down six superstitious pictures, and gave order to take down eighteen cherubims, and to level the chancel.

29. RUSHMERE, Jan. the 27th. We brake down the pictures of the seven deadly sins, and the Holy Lamb with a cross about it, and fifteen other superstitious pictures.

a Vide No. 124, Depredations continued.

30. CHATSHAM, Jan. the 29th. Nothing to be done.

31. WASHBROOK, Jan. the 29th. I broke down twenty-six superstitious pictures, and gave order to take down a stoneing cross, and the chancel to be levelled.

32. COPDOCK, Jan. the 29th. I brake down one hundred and fifty superstitious pictures; two of God the Father, and two crucifixes; did deface a cross on the font, and gave order to take down a stoneing cross on the chancel, and to levell the steps; and took up a brass inscription, with *ora pro nobis,* and *cujus animæ propitietur Deus.*

33. BELSTEAD. We brake down seven superstitious pictures, the Apostles and two others, and took up four inscriptions in brass of *ora pro nobis,* &c.

34. IPSWICH, Stoke Mary's. Two crosses in wood, and two cherubims painted, and one inscription in brass, with *ora pro nobis,* &c.

35. At Peter's, was on the porch, the crown of thorns, the spunge and nails, and the Trinity in stone; and the rails were there, which I gave order to break in pieces.

36. Mary's at the Key, Jan. the 29th. I brake down six superstitious pictures.

37. St. Mary Elmes, Jan. the 29th. There was four iron crosses on the steeple, which they promised to take down that day or the next.

38. Nicholas, Jan. the 29th. We brake six superstitious pictures, and took up two brass inscriptions of *ora pro nobis;* and gave order for another, *cujus animæ propitietur Deus;* and there was the crown of thorns.

39. Mathew's, Jan. the 29th. We brake down thirty-five superstitious pictures, three Angels with stars on their breasts, and crosses.

40. Mary's at the Tower, Jan. the 29th. We took up six brass inscriptions, with *ora pro nobis*, and *ora pro animabus*, and *cujus animæ propitietur Deus;* and pray for the soul, in English; and I gave order to take down five iron crosses, and one of wood on the steeple.

41. Margarett's Jan. the 30th. There was twelve Apostles in stone taken down, and between twenty and thirty superstitious pictures to be taken down, which (a godly man) a churchwarden promised to do.

42. Steven's, Jan. the 30th. There was a popish inscription in brass, " Pray for the soul."

43. Lawrence, Jan. the 30th. There was two popish inscriptions, one with beads, and written *ora pro nobis.*

44. Clements, Jan. the 30th. They four days before had beaten up divers superstitious inscriptions.

45. At [b] Elms, Jan the 30th. Nothing.

b Quere. St. Helens.

46. Playford, Jan. the 30th. We brake down seventeen popish pictures, one of God the Father, and took up two superstitious inscriptions in brass; and one *ora pro nobis*, and *cujus animæ propitietur Deus*, and a second, " Pray for the soul."

47. Blakenham, at the water, Feb. the 1st, 1643. Only the steps to be levelled, which I gave them eight days to do it.

48. Bramford, Feb. the 1st. A cross to be taken off the steeple: we brake down eight hundred and forty-one superstitious pictures; and gave order to take down the steps, and gave a fortnight's time; and took up three inscriptions, with *ora pro nobis*, and *cujus animæ propitietur Deus*.

49. Sproughton. We brake down sixty-one superstitious pictures, and gave order for the steps to be levelled in a fortnight's time; and three inscriptions, *ora pro nobis*, and *cujus animæ propitietur Deus*.

50. Burstall, Feb. the 1st. We took off an iron cross off the steeple, and gave order to levell the steps.

51. Hintlesham, Feb. the 1st. We brake down fifty-one superstitious pictures, and took up three inscriptions, with *ora pro nobis*, and *cujus animæ propitietur Deus;* and gave order for digging down the steps.

52. Hadleigh, Feb. the 2nd. We brake down

thirty superstitious pictures, and gave order for taking down the rest, which were about seventy; and took up an inscription, *quorum animabus propitietur Deus*, and gave order for the taking down a cross on the steeple; gave fourteen days.

53. LAYHAM, Feb. the 2nd. We brake down six superstitious pictures, and take down a cross off the steeple.

54. SHELLY, Feb. the 2nd. We brake down six superstitious pictures, and took off two inscriptions, with *cujus animæ propitietur Deus*.

55. HIGHAM, Feb. the 2nd. We brake down fifteen superstitious pictures in the chancel, and sixteen in the church, (so called,) and gave order to levell the steps in fourteen days.

56. Feb. the 3d. WENHAM Magna. There was nothing to reform.

57. Feb. the 3d. WHENHAM Parva. We brake down twenty-six superstitious pictures, and gave order to break down six more, and to levell the steps: one picture was of the Virgin Mary.

58. Feb. the 3d. CAPELL. We break down three superstitious pictures, and gave order to take down thirty-one, which the churchwarden promised to do; and to take down a stoneing cross on the outside of the church (as it is called.)

Feb. the 3d. We were at the Lady Bruce's house, and in her chapel; there was a picture of God the Father, of the Trinity, of Christ, and the

Holy Ghost, the cloven tongues, which we gave order to take down, and the lady promised to do it.

59. NEEDHAM-MARKET, Feb. the 5th. We gave order to take down two iron crosses on the chappel and a stoneing cross.

60. BADLEY, Feb. the 5th. We brake down thirty-four superstitious pictures; Mr. Dove promised to take down the rest, twenty-eight, and to levell the chancel. We took down four superstitious inscriptions, with *ora pro nobis*, and *cujus animæ propitietur Deus*.

61. STOW-MARKET, Feb. the 5th. We gave order to break down about seventy superstitious pictures, and to levell the chancel, to Mr. Manning, that promised to do it; and to take down two crosses, one on the steeple, and the other on the church, (as it is called,) and took up an inscription of *ora pro nobis*.

62. WETHERDEN, Feb. the 5th. We brake a hundred superstitious pictures in Sr Edward Silliard's Isle, and gave order to break down sixty more, and to take down sixty-eight cherubims, and to levell the steps in the chancel; there was taken up nineteen superstitious inscriptions that weighed sixty-five pounds.

63. ELMSWELL, Feb. the 5th. We brake down twenty superstitious pictures, and gave order to break down forty and above, and to take down

forty cherubims. We took up four superstitious inscriptions with *ora pro nobis*.

64. TOSTICK, Feb. the 5th. We brake down about sixteen superstitious pictures, and gave order to take down about forty more, and to levell the steps. We took up a superstitious inscription with *ora pro nobis*.

65. BURY ST. EDMUND's, Feb. the 5th. Mary's Parish. Mr. Chaplain undertook to do down the steps, and to take away the superstitious pictures.

66. James's Parish. Mr. Moody undertook for.

67. KINFORD, Feb. the 6th. We gave order to take down a cross and other pictures.

68. Feb. the 6th. At NEWMARKET. They promised to amend all.

69. COMEARTH Magna, Feb. the 20th. I took up two inscriptions, " Pray for our souls," and gave order to take down a cross on the steeple, and to levell the steps. John Pain, churchwarden, for not paying, and doing his duty injoined by the ordinance, I charged Henry Turner, the constable, to carry him before the Earl of Manchester.

70. Little COMEARTH, Feb. the 20th. There were two crosses, one in wood and another in stone, which I gave order to take them down; and I brake down six superstitious pictures. Had no noble.

71. NEWTON, Feb. the 21st. William Plume, churchwarden, and John Shrive, constable. I

brake down four superstitious pictures, one of Christ, and six in the chancel, one of Christ and one of the the Virgin Mary; and to see the steps levelled.

^cNAYLAND, Feb. the 21st. Henry Hill, Henry Campin, churchwardens; Abraham Vangover, constable. Churchwardens promised the 6s. 8d. within a week.

72. ASSINGTON, Feb. the 21st. We brake down forty pictures, one of God the Father, and the other very superstitious; and gave order to levell the chancel, and to take a cross off the steeple. Constable, James Springes.

73. At Mr. Thomas Humberfield's or Somberfield's. I brake down nine superstitious pictures and a crucifix in the Parish of STOKE. He refused to pay the 6s. 8d. This was in the Lord Windsor's chappel.

74. Feb. the 23d. At Mr. Capt. Waldgrave's chappel, in BUERS, there was a picture of God the Father, and divers other superstitious pictures, twenty at least, which they promised to break, his daughter and servants; he himself was not at home, neither could they find the key of the chappel. I had not the 6s. 8d. yet promised it; and gave order to take down a cross.

75. BUERS, Feb. the 23d. We brake down above six hundred superstitious pictures, eight

c Vide No. 7.

Holy Ghosts, three of God the Father, and three of the Son. We took up five inscriptions of *quorum animabus propitietur Deus*, one " Pray for the soul:" and superstitions in the windows, and some divers of the Apostles.

76. COMEARTH, Magna. (Mentioned at No. 69.)

77. GLENSFORD, Feb. the 26th. We brake down many pictures; one of God the Father, a picture of the Holy Ghost, in brass. A noble.

78. OTLEY, Feb. the 27th. A deputy brake down fifty superstitious pictures, a cross on the chancel, two brass inscriptions, and Moses with a rod, and Aaron with his mitre taken down; and twenty cherubims to be broke down.—*6s. 8d.*

79. MULLEDEN, Feb the 27th. He brake down six superstitious pictures, and gave order to levell the steps in twenty days.—*6s. 8d.*

80. HOO, Feb. the 27th. A superstitious inscription of brass, and eight superstitious pictures brake down, and gave order to levell the steps in twenty days.—*6s. 8d.*

81. ^eLETHERINGHAM, Feb. the 27. He took up three popish inscriptions of brass, and brake

---

e The present ruinous condition of this church, together with the numerous and once beautiful monuments of the ancient families of the Wingfields and Nauntons, is much to be lamented. To prevent their being wholly lost to posterity, it is with pleasure we announce that correct and elegant drawings of the whole of the monuments were taken, in 1785, by Mr. Isaac Johnson, by order of the Antiquarian Society.

down ten superstitious pictures, and gave order to levell the steps in twenty days.—*6s. 8d.*

82. EASTON, Feb. the 28th. He brake up one inscription in brass, and sixteen superstitious pictures, three crosses he gave order to take down, and to levell the steps in twenty days.—*6s. 8d.*

83. KETTLEBURGH, Feb. the 28th. In the glass six superstitious pictures; gave order to break them down, and to levell the steps in twenty days.—*6s. 8d.*

84. HELMINGHAM, Feb. the 29th. Brake down three superstitious pictures, and gave order to take down four crosses and nine pictures, and Adam and Eve to be beaten down.—*6s. 8d.*

85. WOOLPIT, Feb. the 29th. My Deputy. Eighty superstitious pictures; some he brake down, and the rest he gave order to take down; and eight crosses to be taken down in twenty days.—*6s. 8d.*

86. BAYTON Bull, March the 1st. He brake down twenty pictures, and the steps to be levelled in twenty days.—*6s. 8d.*

87. KAYFIELD, April the 3d. A Deputy brake down divers, which I have done.

88. April the 3d. BEDDINGFIELD. I brake down fourteen superstitious pictures; one of God the Father, and two doves, and another of St. Catherine and her wheel; and gave order to take down three stoneing crosses on porch, church, and chancel.

89. TANNINGTON, April the 3d. My Deputy brake down twenty-seven pictures; two were crucifixes, which I brake of part.

90. BRUNDISH, April the 3d. There were five pictures of Christ, the twelve Apostles, a crucifix, and divers superstitious pictures. The Vicar have two livings.

91. WILBY, April the 4th. Forty superstitious pictures. Thirty we brake down, and gave order to take ten more and the steps to be levelled; and the whip, and pincers, and nails that was at Christ's crucifying, and the Trinity, all in stone.

92. STRADBROOK, April the 4th. Eight Angels off the roof, and cherubims in wood, to be taken down; and four crosses on the steeple, and one on the church, and one on the porch, and seventeen pictures on the upper window, and "Pray for such out of your charity," and organs, which I brake.

93. Nether, or LINSTEAD Parva, April the 4th. A picture of God the Father, and of Christ, and five more superstitious in the chancel, and the steps to be levelled, which the churchwardens promised to do in twenty days; and a picture of Christ on the outside of the steeple nailed to a cross, and another superstitious one. Crosses on the font. Will. (MS. blotted) is Curate.

94. LINSTEAD Magna, April the 5th. Here was two superstitious *orate pro animabus*, and *cujus animæ propitietur Deus*. There was two crucifixes,

and eight superstitious pictures, and three inscriptions of Jesus in a window; and gave order to levell the steps to Mr. Evered, Will. Aldice, Curate, D******* Francis Evered.

95. Cheston, or CHEDISTON, April the 5th. Two superstitious inscriptions and seven popish pictures, one of Christ and another of St. George. —6s. 8d.

96. HALLISWORTH, April the 5th. Two crucifixes, three of the Holy Ghost, and a third of the Trinity altogether, and two hundred other superstitious pictures and more; five popish inscriptions of brass, *orate pro animabus*, and *cujus animæ propitietur Deus*, and the steps to be levelled by the Parson of the town, and to take off a cross on the chancel. And then the churchwardens had order to take down two crosses off the steeple.

97. REDSHAM Magna, April the 5th. A crucifix and three other superstitious pictures; and gave order for Mr. Barenby the Parson, to levell the steps in the chancel. He preach but once a day.

98. REGINFIELD, April the 5th. The sun and moon, and JESUS in capital letters, and two crosses on the steeple; we gave order to take them down and levell the steps in fourteen days.

99. BECCLES, April the 6th. Jehovah's between church and chancel, and the sun over it; and by the altar, "My meat is flesh indeed, and My blood is drink indeed," and two crosses we gave

order to take down, one was on the porch, another on the steeple, and many superstitious pictures, about forty. Six several crosses, Christ's, Virgin Mary's, St. George's, and three more, and thirteen crosses in all; and Jesus and Mary in letters, and the twelve Apostles.

100. ELOUGH, April the 6th. We brake down twelve superstitious pictures, and the steps to be levelled, and a cross to be taken off the chancel, which they promised to do.

101. SATERLY. There was divers superstitious pictures painted, which they promised to take down; and I gave order to levell the steps, and to break in pieces the rails, which I have seen done; and to take off a cross on the church.

102. BENACRE, April the 6th. There was six superstitious pictures, one crucifix, and the Virgin Mary twice, with Christ in her arms, and Christ lying in the manger, and the three kings coming to Christ with their presents, and St. Catherine twice pictured; and the Priest of the Parish— (MS. blotted)—*materna ^{f} Johannem Christi guberna*, "O Christ, govern me by thy mother's prayers!" And three bishops with their mitres, and the steps to be levelled within six weeks; and eighteen JESUS'S written in capital letters on the roof, which we gave order to do out, and the story of Nebuchadnezzar, and *orate pro animabus* in a glass window.

f Sic MS.

103. COCHIE, April the 6th. We brake down two hundred pictures; one pope, with divers cardinals, Christ and the Virgin Mary; a picture of God the Father, and many other which I remember not. There was four steps with a valt underneath, but the two first might be levelled, which we gave order to the churchwardens to do. There was many inscriptions of JESUS in capital letters on the roof of the church, and cherubims with crosses on their breasts, and a cross in the chancel, all which, with divers pictures in the windows, which we could not reach, neither would they help us to raise the ladders; all which we left a warrant with the constable to do in fourteen days.

104. RUSHMERE, April the 8th. We brake ten superstitious pictures, and gave order to levell the steps in twenty days, to brake their windows; and we brake down a pot for holy water.

105. MUTFORD, April the 8th. We brake down nine superstitious pictures, and gave order to take up nine superstitious inscriptions of Jesus, two crosses on the steeple, and the steps to be levelled.

106. FROSTENDEN, April the 8th. Twenty superstitious pictures, one crucifix, and a picture of God the Father, and St. Andrew with his cross, and St. Catherine with her wheel; four cherubims on the pulpit, two crosses on the steeple, and one on the chancel. And Mr. Ellis, an high constable of the town, told me, " he saw an Irish man, within

two months, bow to the cross on the steeple, and put off his hat to it." The steps were there to levell, which they promised to do.

107. COE, April the 8th. We took down forty-two superstitious pictures in glass, and above twenty cherubims, and the steps we have digged down.

108. RAYDEN, April the 8th. We brake down ten superstitious pictures, and gave order to take down two crosses, one on the chancel, and another on the porch. Steps we digged up.

109. SOUTHWOLD, April the 8th. We brake down one hundred and thirty superstitious pictures; St. Andrew, and four crosses on the four corners of the vestry; and gave order to take down thirteen cherubims, and take down twenty angels, and to take down the cover of the font.

110. WALBERWICK. Brake down forty superstitious pictures, and to take off five crosses on the steeple and porch; and we had eight superstitious inscriptions on the grave-stones.

111. BLYFORD, April the 9th. There was thirty superstitious pictures, a crucifix, and the four Evangelists, and the steps promised to be levelled, and begun to be digged down; a cross on the chancel they promised to take down, and a triangle on the porch, for the Trinity, and two whips, &c. Christ and a cross all over the porch.

112. BLYBOROUGH, April the 9th. There was

twenty superstitious pictures; one on the outside of the church; two crosses, one on the porch, and another on the steeple; and twenty cherubims to be taken down in the church and chancel; and I brake down three *orate pro animabus*, and gave order to take down above two hundred more pictures within eight days.

113. DUNWICH, April the 9th. At Peter's Parish. Sixty-three cherubims, sixty at least of JESUS written in capital letters on the roof, and forty superstitious pictures, and a cross on the top of the steeple: all was promised by the churchwardens to be done.

114. Allhallows. Thirty superstitious pictures, and twenty-eight cherubims, and a cross on the chancel.

115. BRAMFIELD, April the 9th. Twenty-four superstitious pictures, one crucifix, and picture of Christ, and twelve Angels on the roof, and divers JESUS'S in capital letters; and the steps to be levelled by Sr Robert Brook.

116. HEVININGHAM, April the 9th and 10th. Eight superstitious pictures, one of the Virgin Mary, and two inscriptions of brass, one "Pray for the soul," and another, *orate pro animabus*.

117. POLSTEAD, April the 15th. Forty-five superstitious pictures; one of Peter with his keys, second a bishop's mitre on his head.—6*s.* 8*d.*

118. BOXTEAD. We had six superstitious pictures.

119. STANSTEAD, April the 15th. Five superstitious pictures.

120. LAXFIELD, July the 17th, 1644. Two Angels in stone at the steeple's end, a cross in the church, and another on the porch in stone, and two superstitious pictures on stone there. Many superstitious inscriptions in brass, *orate pro animabus et cujus animæ propitietur Deus.* A picture of Christ in glass; an eagle, and a lion with wings, for two of the evangelists, and the steps in the chancel; all to be done within twenty days; the steps by William Dowsing of the same town.

121. TREMBLY, Aug. the 21st. 1644. Martin's. There was a fryar with a shaven crown praying to God in these words, *miserere mei Deus*, which we brake down; and twenty-eight cherubims in the church, which we gave order to take down by Aug. 24th.

122. Aug. the 21st. BRIGHTWELL. A picture of Christ and the Virgin Mary, that we brake down, and the twelve Apostles painted in wood, and a holy water font, and a step to be levelled; all which we gave order to be broke down, and the steps to be levelled, by Aug. 31st.

123. LEVINGTON, Aug. the 21st. The steps only to be levelled by Aug. 31st, and a double cross on the church.

124. UFFORD, Aug. 31st. (See No. 26.) where is set down what we did Jan. the 27th. "Thirty

superstitious pictures, and left thirty-seven more to break down," and some of them we brake down now. In the chancel we brake down an Angel, three *orate pro anima* in the glass, and the Trinity in a triangle, and twelve cherubims on the roof of the chancel, and nigh a hundred JESUS—MARIA in capital letters, and the steps to be levelled. And we brake down the organ cases, and gave them to the poor. In the church there was on the roof above a hundred JESUS and MARY in great capital letters, and a crosier staff to be broke down in glass, and above twenty stars on the roof. There is a glorious cover over the font, like a pope's tripple crown, with a pelican on the top picking its breast, all gilt over with gold. And we were kept out of the church above two hours, and neither churchwardens, William Brown nor Roger Small, that were enjoined these things above three months afore, had not done them in May; and I sent one of them to see it done, and they would not let him have the key. And now, neither the churchwardens nor William Brown, nor the constable, James Tokelove, and William Gardener, the sexton, would not let us have the key in two hours time. New churchwardens, Thomas Stanard, Thomas Stroud; and Samuel Canham, of the same town, said, " I sent men to rifle the church:" and Will. Brown, old churchwarden said, " I went about to pull down the church, and had carried away part of the church."

125. BAYLHAM. There was the Trinity in a triangle on the font, and a cross; and the steps to be levelled by the minister in twenty-one days.

126. NETTLESTEAD, Aug. the 22d. An inscription in the church in brass, *orate pro anima*, and six of the Apostles, not defaced; and St. Catherine with her wheel, and three superstitious pictures more, two with crosier staves, with mitres, and the picture of St. George, St. Martin, and St. Simon.

127. SUMMERSHAM, the same day. A cross in the glass, and St. Catherine with her wheel, and another picture in the glass in the church; and two superstitious pictures in the window, and a holy water font in the church, and on the outside of the chancel door, Jesus. *Sancta Maria*. Jesus.

128. FLOUGHTON, Aug. the 22d. A holy water font in the chancel.

129. ELMSETT, Aug. the 22d. Crow, a Deputy, had done before we came. We rent a-pieces there the hood and surplice.

130. OFTON, Aug. the 22d. There was a holy water font in the chancel, and the steps, and some crosses on the outside of the church and chancel; and we gave order to deface them. We gave order to have them all defaced, and two more in a window of the church, and two stone crosses on the top of the steeple: all which we gave order to mend all the defaults by Saturday come 'sennight. At Ipswich, at Mr. Coley's.

131. BARKING. Aug. the 21st. There was St. Catherine with her wheel. Many superstitious pictures were done afore I came. There was Maria's on the church door.

123. WILLESHAM, Aug. the 22d. An holy water font in the chancel; the steps were levelled, and had been so once before by a lord bishop's injunction, and by another lord bishop after commanded; testified to me by him that saw it done, Mr. John Brownbridge.

133. DAMSDEN, Aug. the 23d. Three crosses in the chancel on the wall, and a holy water font there, and the chancel to be levelled by Saturday s'ennight after.

134. WETHERINGSETT, Aug. the 26th. Nineteen crosses; sixteen about the arches of the church, and three on the porch; a picture on the porch, a triangle for the Trinity, to be done. Thomas Colby and Thomas Eley, churchwardens. Constables, John Suton and John Genkthorne.

135. MICKFIELD, Aug. the 26th. Two crosses, and the glasses to be made up by Saturday come three weeks. And 10s. to be paid to the poor within that time, and the rest afterwards.—4s. 6d.

136. HORHAM, Aug. the 27th. In the chancel a holy water font, and the steps to be levelled; and there was the four evangelists, and a part of a crucifix, and divers angels, eight, and other superstitious pictures; and *orate pro animabus*; and, on

a grave stone, *cujus animæ propitietur Deus.* All which I brake up, and gave twenty days to levell the steps and make the windows. And in the church *orate pro animabus* and divers superstitious pictures, and a triangle on the font, and a superstitious picture.—6*s.* 8*d.*

137. ALLINGTON, Aug. the 27th. In the chancel was Peter pictured, and crucified with his heels upward, and there was John Baptist and ten more superstitious pictures in the church.

138. WALLINGWORTH, Aug. the 27th. A stone cross on the top of the church, three pictures of Adam on the porch, two crosses on the font, and a triangle for the Trinity in stone, and two other superstitious pictures, and the chancel ground to be levelled; and the holy water font to be defaced, and step levelled in fourteen days. Edward Dunstone and John ———, constables. William Dod and Robert Bemant, churchwardens.—3*s.* 4*d.*

139. HOLTON, by Halesworth, Aug. the 29th. Two superstitious pictures in the church, and I. H. S., the Jesuit's badge, in the chancel window; promised by the minister, Mr. Wm. Pell.

140. WANGFORD, Aug. the 28th. Sixteen superstitious pictures, and one I brake. Fourteen still remain, and one of God.

141. WRENTHAM, Aug. the 28th. Twelve superstitious pictures, one of St. Catherine with her wheel.

142. HOXNE, Aug. the 30th. Two stone crosses on church and chancel, Peter with his fish, and a cross in a glass window, and four superstitious ones. The Virgin Mary with Christ in her arms, and cherubims wings on the font. Many more were broken down afore.

143. EYE, Aug. the 30th. Seven superstitious pictures in the chancel, and a cross, one was Mary Magdalene, all in the glass, and six in the church windows; many more had been broke down afore.

144. OCKOLD, Aug. Divers superstitious pictures were broke. I came, and there was Jesus, Mary, and St. Lawrence with his gridiron, and Peter's keys. Churchwardens promised to send 5s. to Mr. Oales before Michaelmas.

145. RUSSINGLES, Aug. the 30th. Nothing but a step. The pictures were broke before.

146. METTFIELD, Aug. the 30th. In the church was Peter's keys and the Jesuit's badge in the window, and many on the top of the roof. I. for Jesus, H. for *Hominum*, and S. for *Salvator*, and a dove for the Holy Ghost in wood, and the like in the chancel; and there, in brass, *orate pro animabus*, and the steps to be levelled by Sept. the 7th. Mr. Jermin, the gentleman in the town, refused to take up the inscription, as the churchwarden informed, whose name is ———.

147. DINNINGTON, Sept. the 26th, 1644. Angels in Sr John Rouse's Isle, and two holy water fonts;

and in Bacon's Isle, nine pictures of Angels and crosses, and a holy water font; and ten superstitious pictures in the chancel, and a holy water font, and two superstitious inscriptions of Christ; the spear and nails on two stools at the lower end of the church, and a cherubim in Sr John Rouse's stool.

148. BADDINGHAM, Sept. the 28th. The steps to be levelled in the chancel, and sixteen superstitious cherubims with crosses on their breasts. All to be done by the churchwardens by the 13th of October.

149. PARHAM-HATCHESTON, Oct. the 1st. There was twenty-one cherubims with wings in wood, and sixteen superstitious pictures and popish saints, with a double cross, in the church; and the representation of the Trinity on the font, and the spears and nails that Christ was pierced and nailed with, and three crosses, all in stone; four superstitious pictures in the chancel, and a cross, all in glass; and the steps to be levelled by Mr. Francis Warner by Oct. 15th. All to be done.

Feb. 4th. By virtue of a Warrant directed to me by the right Honble the Earl of Manchester. I do hereby depute and appoint you, T. D., in my absence, to execute the said warrant in every particular, within the County of ———, according to an ordinance of Parliament therein mentioned, and power given unto me by the said Warr⁺ as fully as I myself may, or might, execute the same. In witness whereof I have hereunto set my hand and seal.

Thomas Umberfield of STOKE refused to pay the 6s. 8d. (See No. 6.)

A crucifix, and divers superstitious pictures, Feb. 21st.

END OF THE MANUSCRIPT.

OXFORD EDITIONS.

		s.	d.
KEBLE'S Selections from HOOKER	18°	5	0
Auto-Biography of Bp. PATRICK	18°	3	6
PATRICK'S Advice to a Friend	18°	3	6
———— Heart's Ease	18°	3	6
———— on Repentance and Fasting	18°	3	6
SUTTON'S Disce Mori	18°	3	6
———— Disce Vivere	18°	3	6
———— Meditations on the Sacrament	18°	3	6
TAYLOR'S [Bp.] Golden Grove	18°	3	6
WILSON'S [Bp.] Sacra Privata	18°	3	6
LAUD'S [Abp.] Devotions	18°	3	6
Auto-Biography of Abp. LAUD	18°	5	0
SPARROW'S Rationale on the Book of Common Prayer	18°	5	0

In the Press.

SARAVIA on the Priesthood.
A KEMPIS' Imitation of Christ.

JOHN HENRY PARKER, OXFORD.

Lightning Source UK Ltd.
Milton Keynes UK
UKHW020821060122
396716UK00007B/554